Dennis the Menace

Ain't Misbehavin'

By HANK KETCHAM

FAWCETT GOLD MEDAL • NEW YORK

"I FINALLY GOT A PITCHER OF MR. WILSON SMILING! I TOLD HIM WE WAS MOVIN' TO ANOTHER PART OF TOWN."

"I'LL BE OUT LATER, JOEY. MY MOM IS MAKIN' STEW. AN' I GOTTA CHECK THE STUFF SHE'S PUTTIN' *IN* IT!"

"*MOM!* OUR NEW PAPER BOY IS A **GIRL**!"

"YOU HUNT OVER THERE, AN' I'LL START LOOKIN' THROUGH THE BUSHES."

"YA CAN'T BELIEVE EVERYTHING YOU HEAR ON TELEBISHION, JOEY..
SOME OF IT'S JUST A LOTTA *CARROT SOUP!*"

"YA THINK YOU **KNOW** PEOPLE. THIS MORNING MY MOM ASKED IF I WASN'T GETTIN' TIRED OF PEANUT BUTTER SAMWICHES FOR LUNCH EVERY DAY!"

"...AN' WHEN YOU'RE **OLD** AND YOU WANNA COME AND LIVE WITH ME, I'LL REMEMBER THIS!"

"YEAH, I'M AN ONLY KID...AND OVER THERE IS MY ONLY MOTHER AND MY ONLY FATHER."

"DID YA EVER EAT A **RAW ONION** SAMWICH, MR. WILSON?"

"*BOY!* SHOES LIKE THIS MAKE YA FEEL FOUR YEARS OLD AGAIN!"

"DON'T **GULP** IT, JOEY... FIRST YOU SNIFF IT, THEN YOU ROLL IT AROUND ON YOUR TONGUE."

"AFRAID I'M NOT THAT KIND
OF A DOCTOR, SON."

"HE WON'T MIND!"

"WOW! YOU MEAN I JUST WON A REAL, LIVE **KANGAROO**?"

"DID YOU HEAR A **SHRIEK** AN' A **THUD**?"

"I NEVER **HEARD** OF VEELSCAPPOLONEY...I BET IT'S **RABBIT** AN' YOU DON'T WANNA *TELL ME!*"

"WHY WOULD I WANTA
MEET YOUR SISTER?"

"MMMM...PLEASED TO
MEETCHA, I'M SURE, LORI!"

"LORI CAN MAKE BROWNIES LIKE YA NEVER TASTED BEFORE!"

"YOU EVER TASTE SPUMONE?"

"HEY! YOU WANTA MEET LORI?"

"YOU CAN SPEAKA THE ENGLISH WHEN YOU *WANT* TO!"

"THERE'S SOMETHIN' I WANTED TO ASK YOU...WHAT WAS ALL THAT *THUNDERIN'* AND *LIGHTNIN'* ABOUT LAST NIGHT?"

"DON'T **NEVER** THROW ROCKS AT AIRPLANES, JOEY! WHEN I GO TO VISIT MY GRAMPA, I'M GONNA BE SITTIN' BY A **WINDOW!**"

"I'VE FLOWN THREE
TIMES ALREADY."

"BROOMS DON'T
COUNT, MARGARET."

"WON'T YOU BE SCARED 'WAY UP THERE?"

"NAW... I FEEL SORRY FOR ANY OLD WITCH THAT GETS IN FRONT OF A 747."

"I'M GONNA VISIT MY GRAMPA ... AN' WHEN WE COME BACK, WE MIGHT HAVE A **PONY** WITH US!"

"WHY CAN'T I BRING
MY DOG?"

"NO TREES."

"WOW! I THINK I CAN SEE CLEAR INTO TOMORROW!"

"WHICH AM I...VACANT OR OCCUPIED?"

"WHICH WAY TO THE POOL?"

"I BEEN WANTIN' A *HORSE* FOR A LONG, LONG TIME... MAYBE YOU CAN HEAR ME A LITTLE BETTER UP HERE."

"WAKE ME UP IF WE SHOULD LAND ON THE MOON... I WOULDN'T WANTA MISS IT."

"YOU'D MAKE A **SWELL** MOM! YOU NEVER GET MAD, OR YELL, OR..."

"JUST ONE MORE HOUR"

"THEY'RE LOTS BIGGER *INSIDE* THAN THEY ARE OUTSIDE, JOEY... I GOT LOST THREE TIMES."

"ONE OF DENNIS' BAD DAYS?"

"NOT AT ALL...DENNIS HAD A **GREAT** DAY!"

"WELL, IF YOU CAN'T FIND ANYTHING TO EAT, YOU BETTER COME OUT BEFORE YOU CATCH COLD."

"YOU'D EAT A LOT, TOO, IF YOUR MOTOR WAS RUNNIN' ALL THE TIME."

"NO...YOU GOTTA SLEEP ON THE **OUTSIDE**, HOTDOG...
YOUR TOENAILS IS TOO SHARP."

"I HEAR THE MITCHELLS ARE GOING TO HAVE A NEW BABY."

"HEAVENS, GEORGE... YOU DIDN'T GIVE ME TIME TO SAY 'APRIL FOOL.'"

"SITTING HAS VERY LITTLE TO DO WITH THIS JOB, MRS. MITCHELL...BABY *RUNNER* IS MORE LIKE IT!"

"YEP, IT MUST BE SPRING....
YOUR CRAB GRASS IS COMIN' UP."

"MR. WILSON IS AWFUL SMART... HE KNOWS HOW TO SAY 'GO HOME' IN SEVEN LANGWIDGES."

"LET'S **BOTH** TELL HER WE HAD THIS FOR LUNCH TODAY."

"WOW...A WHOLE SPOONFUL! GOOD THING IT WAS JUST **CARROTS**, HUH, MOM?'

"YOU NEVER DID ANYTHING LIKE **THAT** BEFORE!"

"I NEVER HAD THE **CHANCE!**"

"MR. WILSON SAYS I'M THE KID MOST LIKELY TO!"

"HE DIDN'T SAY WHAT..."

"HEAR THAT NOISE, DAD? THAT'S THE SOUND OF EIGHT LADIES TALKIN' AND NOBODY LISTENIN'!"

"SHE'S STILL PRETTY MAD...IF I WAS YOU, I'D BRING HOME **TWO** BOXES OF CANDY."

"I **AM** GIVIN' YOU THE RIGHT ANSWERS! YOU'RE JUST ASKIN' THE WRONG QUESTIONS."

"WHAT COULD BE BETTER THAN PEANUT BUTTER SAMWICHES?"

"LUNCH MONEY."

"I LIKE TO S'PRISE MR. WILSON WHEN HE THINKS HE'S
GOT EVERYTHING LOCKED UP TIGHT."

"YOUR ENGLISH IS COMIN' ALONG REAL GOOD, GINA...I
UNDERSTOOD ALMOST EVERYTHING YOU CALLED HIM."

":GOSH, MOM ... IF I HAD A RABBIT, *NOTHIN'* WOULD GO TO WASTE AROUND HERE!"

"THESE ARE FROM ME AN' MR. WILSON,
BUT HE DON'T KNOW IT YET."

"BOY, IS SHE MAD AT YOU FOR LEAVING YOUR TOOLS OUT WHERE I COULD GET 'EM."

"ISN'T IT NICE THAT NEITHER ONE OF US HAS TO GO TO WORK?"

"IT'S A **DEAL**... I WON'T SING ROCK-A-BYE BABY, AND YOU'LL GO STRAIGHT TO BED AT 9 O'CLOCK."

"I'VE RAISED **TWELVE** LIKE YOU...HOW DO YOU THINK
I GOT TO BE A LITTLE OLD LADY?"

"I THINK MR. WILSON IS CRACKIN' UP! I AST HIM WHAT HE WAS DOIN' AND HE SAID HE WAS FEEDIN' HIS **GRASS!**"

"DON'T BE AFRAID TO BITE INTO ONE...
IT WON'T GO TO WASTE."

"TOO BAD YOU MISSED MY MOM'S CARD PARTY YESTERDAY...
A LOT OF IT WAS ABOUT YOU."

"THANKS, MILLIE, BUT I THINK WE'LL STAY HOME TONIGHT.
GEORGE HAD ONE OF HIS DENNIS DAYS AGAIN."

"MOST OF IT WAS PRETTY DUMB, BUT THAT WAS A **GREAT** FINISH, MARGARET!"

"THEY LOOK LIKE WEEDS TO ME, TOO, JOEY...BUT MY MOM
SAYS THEY'RE LOTS PRETTIER THAN ANY OLD ROSES."

"GUESS WHAT HAD A NERVOUS BREAKDOWN AND HAD TO BE TOWED TO THE GARAGE?"

"I GOT RID OF THE WATER, BUT THE MUD JUST **SITS** THERE!"

"I USED TO GET A *REWARD* FOR EATIN' THIS STUFF! ARE WE RUNNIN' OUT OF MONEY?"

"YOU KNOW THAT VASE YOU ALWAYS WORRY ABOUT, THAT GOT CRACKED? WELL, YOU DON'T HAVE TO WORRY ABOUT IT NO MORE."

"OKAY, KID, YOU'VE HAD YOUR 'ONE LITTLE PEEK'...
NOW GET *OUTA* HERE AND LET ME DO MY WORK!"

"BUT IF YOU'D JUST TRY IT *ONCE*, MOM! IT'S MORE FUN THAN YOU THINK!"

"ME AN' MOM ARE WATCHIN' A MOVIE ON TV...SHE'S DOIN' THE CRYIN' AND I'M EATIN' THE POPCORN."

"HE'S SORRY HE PULLED YOUR HAIR WHILE YOU WAS ROLLER-SKATIN'...AND NOW HE WANTS TO BE FRIENDS."

"WHEN I WAS A KID, I COULD GET **SICK** FOR FIFTY CENTS!"

"WHOA! LET YOUR MOM CALL YOU A COUPLA MORE
TIMES....YOU DON'T WANTA 'SPOIL HER.'"

"YOU'RE RIGHT, JOEY... SHE **DOES** SOUND A LITTLE LIKE A COYOTE HOWLIN' AT THE MOON."

"I LIKE IT BETTER WHEN YOU SMELL OF
FLOUR AN' **VANILLA!**"

"AND WHEN HIS TAIL LOOKS LIKE A QUESTION MARK, IT MEANS 'WHEN DO WE EAT?' "

"Y'KNOW, IF I DON'T GET A HORSE PRETTY SOON, THESE BOOTS IS GONNA WEAR **OUT**!"

"MAYBE IF YOU HEAR THIS PITIFUL MEOW, YOU'LL SET UP AN' FIX BREAKFAST."

"LOOK AT IT THIS WAY, JOEY. GETTIN' A BOOSTER SHOT IS BETTER'N GETTIN' A BAD CASE OF **BOOSTERS**, ISN'T IT?"

"I FINALLY FIGGERED OUT THE BIG HAND AN' THE LITTLE HAND...
AND NOW YOU SWITCH OVER TO *CLICKIN' NUMBERS!*"

"Isn't it funny, Mr. Wilson? All these years and ol' Ruff is **STILL** tryin' to figger you out."

"It's gonna be an ol' swimmin' hole...and it won't cost you a **DIME!**"

"I DON'T *WANTA* GO
OUTSIDE AN' PLAY...

...UNLESS SHE SAYS I *CAN'T.*"

"OKAY, I GIVE UP... WHERE DID YA HIDE THAT OL' CHICKEN LEG?"

"THE IDEA IS TO **CATCH** IT, JOEY... NOT TRY
TO GUESS WHERE IT'S GONNA GO."

"IF I HAVE TO SIT IN THE CORNER FOR SAYIN' IT, AT LEAST YOU COULD TELL ME WHAT IT *MEANS!*"

"IF THIS IS A WRONG NUMBER, WHY
DID YOU ANSWER THE PHONE, MR. WILSON?"

"...WITH MAYBE A LITTLE WHIP CREAM AN' A CHERRY? HUH?"

"WHEN SHE DON'T ANSWER, THAT MEANS DON'T ASK."

"ISN'T THERE SOME WAY WE CAN GET MARGARET A KID OF HER *OWN* TO BOSS AROUND?"

"I CAN'T STAY, MR. WILSON... I JUST COME OVER TO BUG YOU A LITTLE BEFORE DINNER."

"EVERYTHING TASTES **SOAPY!**" "GUESS WHO SAID A *VERY* BAD WORD TODAY?"

"THEY BEEN GETTIN' ALONG LOTS BETTER SINCE THEY STARTED TAKIN' CATNAPS TOGETHER."

"TAKE A PUFF ON
THIS ONE, JOEY."

: "AND THAT'S JUST *AIR!*"

"If you an' Dad are gonna fight, how about makin' some popcorn first?"

"I LIKED TELEBISHION BETTER WHEN I COULDN'T TELL
THE COMMERCIALS FROM THE PROGRAMS."

"THOSE DARK CLOUDS ARE THE FULL ONES COMIN' IN
AND THE WHITE ONES ARE EMPTIES GOIN' **OUT**."

"DON'T NEVER HOLD A GRUDGE, JOEY....JUST *BELT 'EM* AND FORGET ABOUT IT."

"HEY, MOM? CAN I GET BACK ON YOUR NERVES
LONG ENOUGH TO GET SOMETHIN' OUT OF MY ROOM?"

"SOME OF THE KIDS' MOTHERS WAS WONDERIN'
WHERE YOU GET SOME OF THE EXPRESSIONS I USE."

"WHICH IS SMARTER...THE GOOD NEWS FIRST, OR
THE BAD NEWS FIRST?"

"THEY DON'T WANT YOU TO UMPIRE, GINA, 'CAUSE THE LAST TIME YOU THREW *EVERYBODY* OUT OF THE GAME!"

"HANG UP, MOM! I GOTTA CALL
DIAL-A-PRAYER... *QUICK!*"

"WELL...IT'S TIME FOR
MY CAN OF CHILI."

"WHO SAID ANYTHING 'BOUT
YOU BEIN' BORN YESTERDAY?"

"ALWAYS MAKIN' UP NEW RULES! NOW MR. WILSON SAYS I CAN'T EVEN *LOOK* AT HIM OVER THE FENCE!"

"NAW...THE TOOTH FAIRY WON'T CARE IF IT GOT KNOCKED OUT
IN A FIGHT. IT ALL PAYS THE SAME."

"DID YOU REMEMBER TO TELL YOUR WIFE THAT I DON'T MUCH CARE FOR CREAM CHEESE SAMWICHES?"

"HERE COMES OL' MARGARET... AND THERE GO THE REST OF OUR COOKIES!"

"WANNA SEE A SNAKE WITH TWO HEADS, MARGARET?"

"RELAX, DAD... I'LL HAVE THAT OL' TYPEWRITER WORKIN' AGAIN IN **NO** TIME!"

"WHAT ARE SOME OF THEM WORDS YOU SAY WHEN YOU CAN'T HIT A GOLF BALL GOOD?"

"I WANNA ASK HIM SOMETHIN'....BUT HOW CAN I
TELL WHEN HE WAKES UP?"

"I GOT 'ER GOIN', DAD! READIN' THE INSTRUCSHUNS JUST SLOWS YA DOWN."

"OH, *THERE* YA ARE, MR. WILSON! THE WAY YOUR PHONE JUST KEPT RINGIN', I THOUGHT FOR A MINUTE YOU MIGHT BE ASLEEP."

"DON'T WORRY ABOUT THE PAPER...
HERE HE COMES WITH *ANOTHER* ONE!"

"I'D KINDA LIKE TO MAKE THIS
PERSON-TO-PERSON...DO YA MIND?"

"IF YA CAN'T GET ANYONE ELSE, TRY MR. WILSON.
I BETCHA HE'D SIT WITH ME FOR A MILLYUN DOLLARS."

"THE BEST PART ABOUT THE FOURTH OF JULY IS THAT IT'S ALREADY HALF WAY TO CHRISTMAS!"

"I BETTER TELL YA NOW THAT IT'S THE STARS AN' STRIPES FOREVER... 'CAUSE AFTER IT STARTS, YOU WON'T BE ABLE TO HEAR ME."

"*NO FAIR!* I'M UPSTAIRS SAVIN' 'LECTRICITY, AND YOU'RE DOWN HERE WATCHIN' TELEBISHION!"

"**WOOPS**! THEY GET A LITTLE FRISKY WHEN YOU BRING 'EM INTO A WARM ROOM."

"JUS' SMELLIN' THE GRASS...WATCHIN' THE MOON...
TALKIN' TO COPS...STUFF LIKE THAT."

"DON'T GOOD INTENSHUNS COUNT FOR NOTHIN' AROUND HERE?"

"YOU CAN LEARN A **LOT** FROM TELEBISHION, JOEY. F'RINSTANCE, BEFORE YOUR MOM CAN PUT YOU IN THE CORNER, SHE HAS TO READ YOU YOUR RIGHTS...AND YA GET ONE PHONE CALL."

"WAIT! WE GOTTA GO BACK! MR. WILSON CAUGHT MARGARET!"

"GINA, LEMME SPLAIN TO YOU WHAT 'SPENDABLE' MEANS."

"HOW COME MY FEET ARE SO CLOSE TO MY HEAD?"

"HOW ABOUT THAT! YOUR HOUSE IS ONLY NINE FROG HOPS FROM MY HOUSE!"

"IT'S OKAY TO GO HOME, DENNIS... A GUY ON TELEVISION JUST SAID THE ZOO GOT THE TIGER BACK IN HIS CAGE!"